WOMEN IN STEM
TEMPLE GRANDIN
ANIMAL WELFARE CHAMPION

by Clara MacCarald

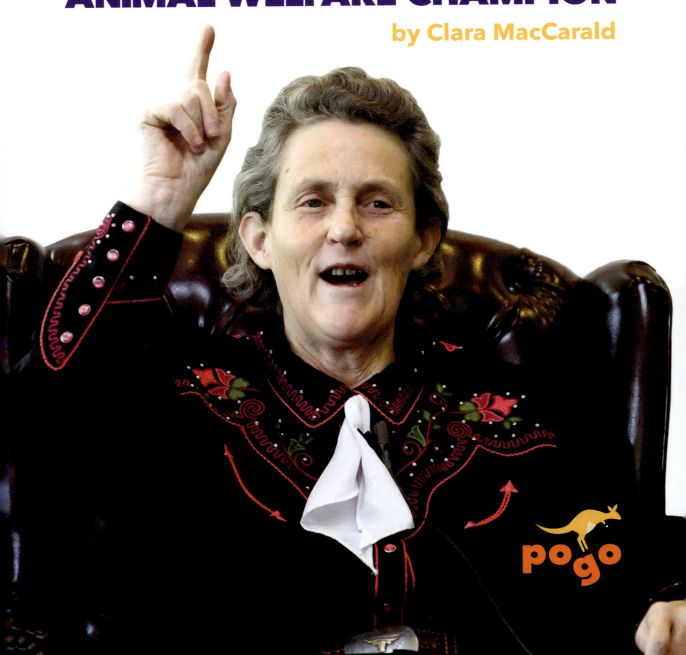

pogo

Ideas for Parents and Teachers

Pogo Books let children practice reading informational text while introducing them to nonfiction features such as headings, labels, sidebars, maps, and diagrams, as well as a table of contents, glossary, and index.

Carefully leveled text with a strong photo match offers early fluent readers the support they need to succeed.

Before Reading

- "Walk" through the book and point out the various nonfiction features. Ask the student what purpose each feature serves.
- Look at the glossary together. Read and discuss the words.

Read the Book

- Have the child read the book independently.
- Invite him or her to list questions that arise from reading.

After Reading

- Discuss the child's questions. Talk about how he or she might find answers to those questions.
- Prompt the child to think more. Ask: Temple Grandin uses science to help animals. How can you use science to make the world a better place?

Pogo Books are published by Jump!
5357 Penn Avenue South
Minneapolis, MN 55419
www.jumplibrary.com

Copyright © 2024 Jump!
International copyright reserved in all countries.
No part of this book may be reproduced in any form without written permission from the publisher.

Library of Congress Cataloging-in-Publication Data

Names: MacCarald, Clara, 1979- author.
Title: Temple Grandin: animal welfare champion / by Clara MacCarald.
Description: Minneapolis, MN: Jump!, Inc., [2024]
Series: Women in STEM | Includes index.
Audience: Ages 7-10
Identifiers: LCCN 2023036558 (print)
LCCN 2023036559 (ebook)
ISBN 9798889967132 (hardcover)
ISBN 9798889967149 (paperback)
ISBN 9798889967156 (ebook)
Subjects: LCSH: Grandin, Temple—Juvenile literature.
Animal scientists—United States—Biography—Juvenile literature.
Autism—Patients—Biography—Juvenile literature.
Classification: LCC SF33.G67 M26 2024 (print)
LCC SF33.G67 (ebook)
DDC 636.0092 [B] —dc23/eng/20230824
LC record available at https://lccn.loc.gov/2023036558
LC ebook record available at https://lccn.loc.gov/2023036559

Editor: Katie Chanez
Designer: Emma Almgren-Bersie

Photo Credits: Nancy Kaszerman/ZUMA Press, Inc./Alamy, cover (foreground); Clara Bastian/iStock, cover (cow); Shutterstock, cover (background); MediaNews Group/Orange County Register/Getty, 1; Eric Isselee/Shutterstock, 3; ©Colorado State University, All Rights Reserved., 4, 14-15; Pictorial Press Ltd/Alamy, 5; Craig Zerbe/Shutterstock, 6; davidf/iStock, 7; Krakenimages.com/Shutterstock, 8-9 (foreground); onurdongel/iStock, 8-9 (background); pabradyphoto/iStock, 10-11; 1968/Shutterstock, 12-13; TZIDO SUN/Shutterstock, 16-17; Kikujiarm/iStock, 18; Nancy Kaszerman/ZUMA Wire/Alamy, 19; Helen H. Richardson/The Denver Post/Getty, 20-21; Oleksandr Lytvynenko/Shutterstock, 23.

Printed in the United States of America at Corporate Graphics in North Mankato, Minnesota.

TABLE OF CONTENTS

CHAPTER 1
Thinking in Pictures................................4

CHAPTER 2
Understanding Animals..........................6

CHAPTER 3
Making Lives Better.............................18

ACTIVITIES & TOOLS
Try This!..22
Glossary..23
Index..24
To Learn More....................................24

CHAPTER 1

THINKING IN PICTURES

Temple Grandin sees the world in a special way. She thinks in pictures instead of words. She notices small things most people do not. She uses her way of looking at the world to help **livestock**.

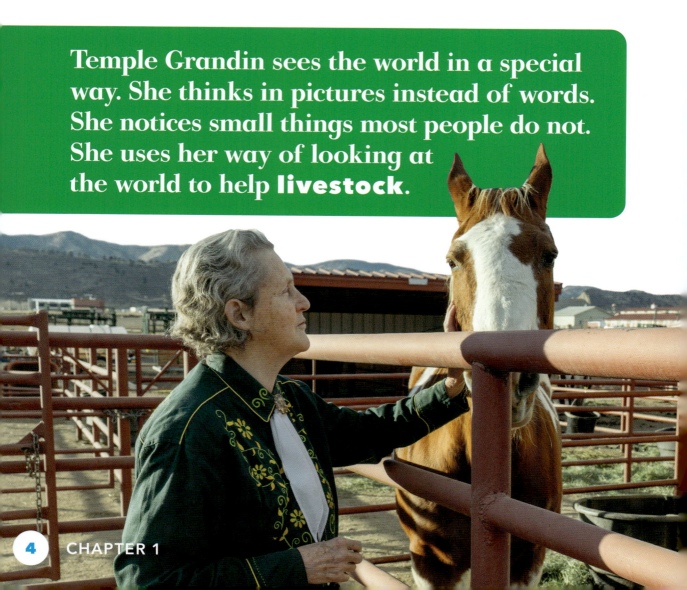

Temple was born in Boston, Massachusetts, in 1947. She did not talk for three years. She was very **sensitive**. Noises bothered her. She didn't like being touched. Doctors **diagnosed** her with **autism**. Being autistic made school hard for Temple. She found it hard to follow written directions. Kids were mean to her.

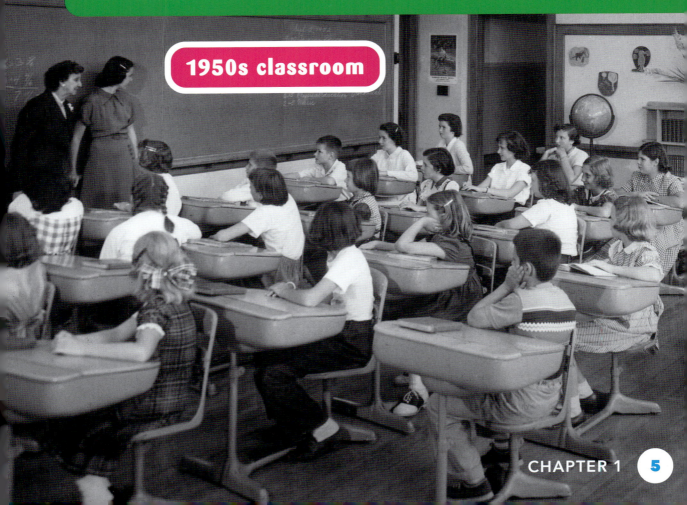

1950s classroom

CHAPTER 1   5

CHAPTER 2
UNDERSTANDING ANIMALS

At age 15, Temple visited her aunt's **ranch**. The cattle were sensitive, too. Sounds and touch often bothered them. Temple **empathized** with them.

Her aunt had squeeze **chutes**. These held cattle tight. They couldn't move away. Her aunt could give them medicine or **vaccines**. Temple noticed something after the cattle were let out. They seemed calmer than before they went in.

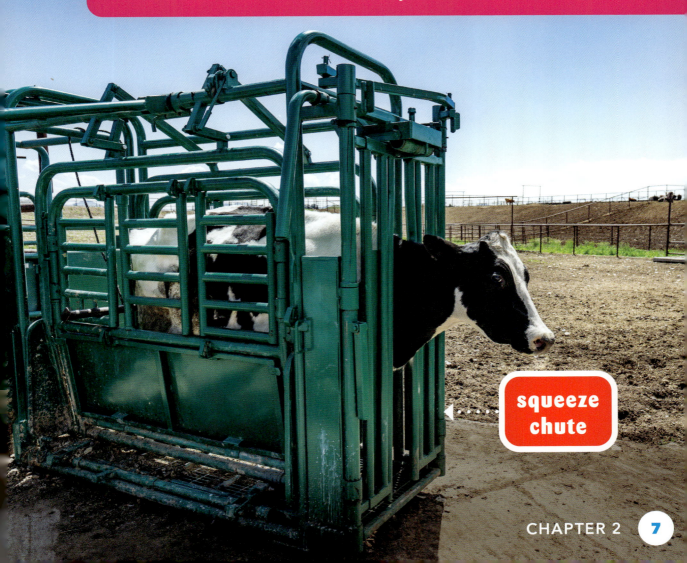

squeeze chute

CHAPTER 2

Temple wondered if squeeze chutes would work for people. In 1965, she invented a new machine. It was like a squeeze chute. But it hugged people. Temple used the hug machine when she felt nervous. Afterward, she felt better.

CHAPTER 2

TAKE A LOOK!

How does Temple's hug machine work? Take a look!

The machine has two big pieces of wood. They have pads for comfort.

A person lies face down between the two pieces of wood.

The person pulls a lever. The lever squeezes the pieces of wood together. They hug the person. The person controls how tight or soft the hug feels.

CHAPTER 2   9

Temple was smart. She went to college. She studied **animal science**. She also started working with livestock on ranches.

In 1990, Temple started teaching animal science. She taught at Colorado State **University**.

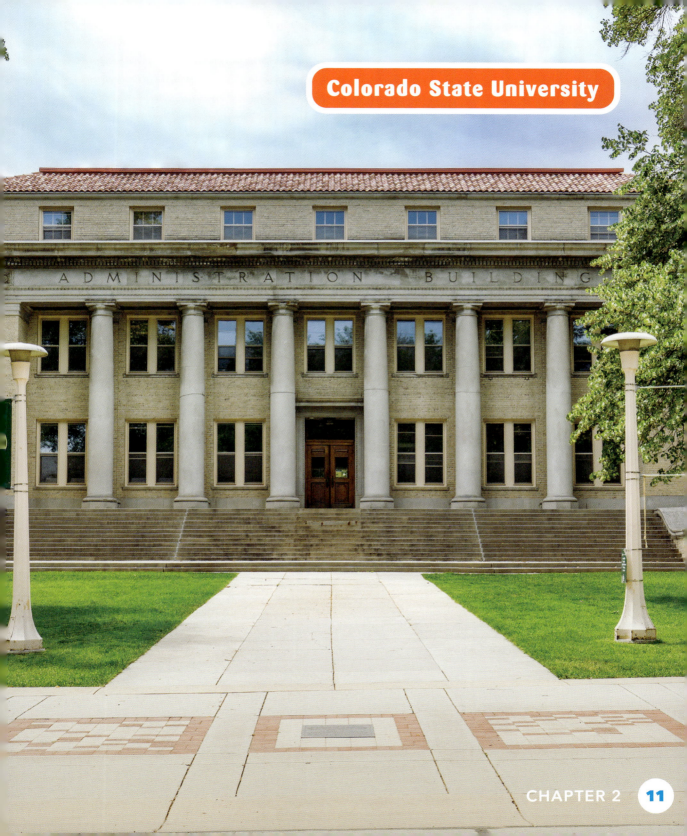

Temple was interested in animal **welfare**. She started by looking at the world the way cattle did. She stood in their pens. She moved through their chutes. She saw problems. Animals can get nervous about things people may not notice. For example, a hanging jacket can look like a **predator**. Temple told ranchers to think about where they left things. She told them to use better floors. Why? Slipping made cattle nervous.

> **DID YOU KNOW?**
>
> Temple knew how animals felt by how they acted. An upset animal might put its ears back. It might make noises. It might sweat.

Chutes are used to move cattle in **slaughterhouses**. Temple noticed these were a big problem for cattle. They could see what happened ahead of them. They got scared. They panicked. They could hurt each other.

Temple invented a new chute. It curved. This way, the cattle couldn't see what happened ahead. They were calmer.

chute

TAKE A LOOK!

How does Temple's chute keep cattle moving? Take a look!

1. Cattle don't like to go toward walls.
2. Cattle like to walk in circles.
3. Cattle like to follow each other.
4. The curves keep cattle from seeing the end of the chute.

CHAPTER 2   15

Temple also made a system to rate, or judge, slaughterhouses. The ratings show how well they treat livestock. Ratings make slaughterhouses better. Why? Companies want to work with slaughterhouses that have good scores.

DID YOU KNOW?

In 1997, McDonald's hired Temple. Why? McDonald's works with slaughterhouses. It asked Temple to make them better places for animals.

CHAPTER 2

CHAPTER 2

CHAPTER 3
MAKING LIVES BETTER

Temple's ideas are used around the world. Many people find her hug machine helpful. Ranchers respect Temple's advice. Her chutes are very popular. Half of the cattle in North America go through machines she invented.

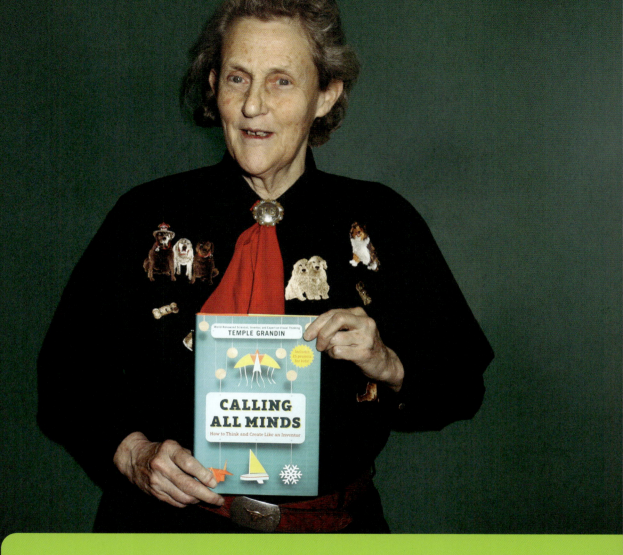

Temple has written books. She writes about autism and animals. In 2018, she wrote a book for children. It is called *Calling All Minds*. It helps readers look at the world and science in different ways.

CHAPTER 3 19

As of 2023, Temple still teaches. She still helps farmers care for animals. She writes and gives talks, too.

Temple also talks about autism. She helps people understand it. She teaches others to value how people with autism think. She continues to do everything she can to make human and animal lives better.

DID YOU KNOW?

A movie was made about Temple's life. It is named after her. It came out in 2010.

CHAPTER 3

ACTIVITIES & TOOLS

TRY THIS!

INVENT TO HELP PETS

Temple made the lives of livestock better by looking at the world the way they did. You can do the same for pets. Try this activity to invent something to make a pet's life better.

What You Need:
- a pet or videos of pets
- paper
- pencil

❶ Watch a pet. If you don't have one, ask a friend or family member if you can watch their pet. Or, you can watch a video of a pet. What is the animal doing? Can you see when it is happy or scared? How can you tell?

❷ Imagine you are the pet. Move around your home. Do you notice anything the pet might enjoy? Is there anything that might scare it?

❸ Could you build something to make the pet happier? What would it be?

❹ Draw a picture of your invention, or write about it. How does it improve the pet's welfare?

GLOSSARY

animal science: The study of the way people raise livestock.

autism: A condition that causes someone to have trouble learning, communicating, and forming relationships with people.

chutes: Narrow walkways.

diagnosed: Determined what disease or condition a person has.

empathized: Understood and shared the emotions and experiences of others.

livestock: Animals kept or raised on a farm or ranch.

predator: An animal that hunts other animals for food.

ranch: A large farm where people raise livestock.

sensitive: Easily bothered by things such as noises and sights.

slaughterhouses: Places where livestock are killed for meat or other products.

university: A place where people study for degrees beyond high school.

vaccines: Drugs that protect people or animals from certain diseases.

welfare: A person or animal's general health and well-being.

INDEX

animal science 10
animal welfare 13
autism 5, 19, 20
Calling All Minds 19
cattle 6, 7, 13, 14, 15, 18
chutes 13, 14, 15, 18
Colorado State University 10
empathized 6
hug machine 8, 9, 18
livestock 4, 10, 16
McDonald's 16
medicine 7
movie 20
pens 13
predator 13
ranch 6, 10
rate 16
school 5, 10
sensitive 5, 6
slaughterhouses 14, 16
squeeze cutes 7, 8
vaccines 7

TO LEARN MORE

Finding more information is as easy as 1, 2, 3.
1. Go to www.factsurfer.com
2. Enter "TempleGrandin" into the search box.
3. Choose your book to see a list of websites.